# Violin II

# SCHIRMER'S LIBRARY
## OF MUSICAL CLASSICS

Vol. 2083

# JOHANN SEBASTIAN BACH

## Violin Concertos

### Concerto for Two Violins in D minor

For Violin and Piano

Edited and fingered
by Eduard Hermann

ISBN 978-1-4234-4182-3

# G. SCHIRMER, Inc.

DISTRIBUTED BY
HAL•LEONARD®
CORPORATION
7777 W. BLUEMOUND RD. P.O. BOX 13819 MILWAUKEE, WI 53213

www.schirmer.com
www.halleonard.com

# Concerto for Two Violins in D minor
## BWV 1043

Edited and Fingered by
Eduard Herrmann

**Violin II**

Johann Sebastian Bach
(1685–1750)

**Vivace**

(The Tutti have to be played)

## Violin II

4

Largo, ma non tanto

(The theme is to be played with a full, soft tone)

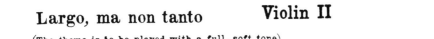

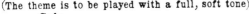

*espressivo*

**A**

*espr.*

*p*

*espressivo*

**B** *a tempo*

**C**

## Violin II

# Violin II

## Violin II

## Violin II

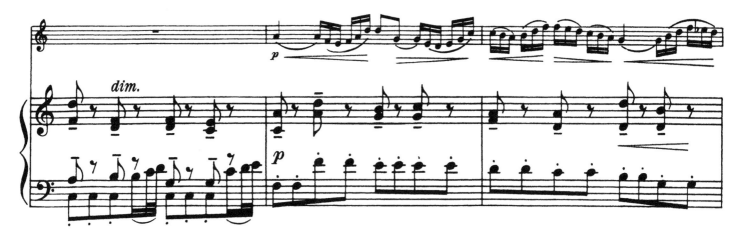

Allegro assai

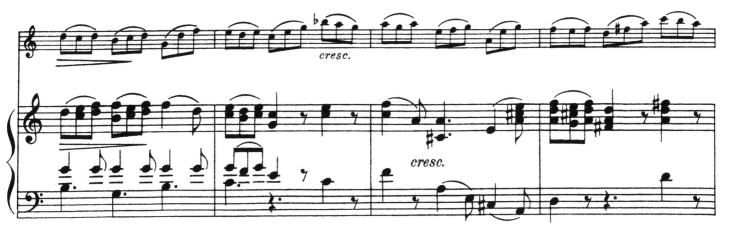

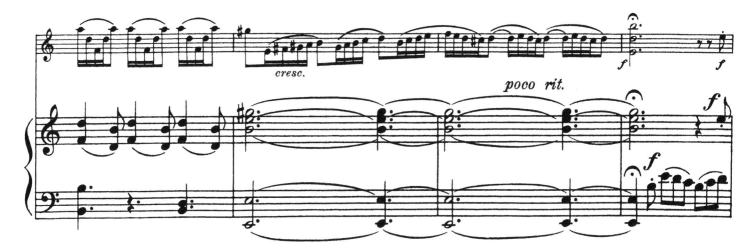

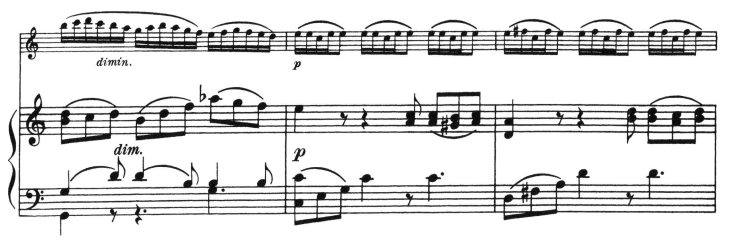

# Concerto for Two Violins in D minor
## BWV 1043

Edited and Fingered by
Eduard Herrmann

Johann Sebastian Bach
(1685–1750)

\* The Violins have to play the Tutti.

**A**

poco dim.

SOLO

without Pedal

poco dim.

cresc.

cresc.

poco dim.

poco dim.

E

**Largo, ma non tanto**

C

D

**Allegro**

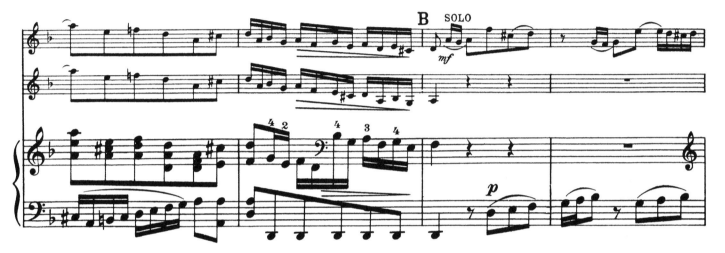